P9-DHE-691

basketball's new wave

Kobe
Bryant

Hard to the Hoop

BY
MARK STEWART

THE MILLBROOK PRESS
BROOKFIELD, CONNECTICUT

M

THE MILLBROOK PRESS

Produced by
BITTERSWEET PUBLISHING
John Sammis, President
and
TEAM STEWART, INC.

Series Design and Electronic Page Makeup by
JAFFE ENTERPRISES
Ron Jaffe

Researched and Edited by Mariah Morgan

All photos courtesy
AP/ Wide World Photos, Inc.,
except the following:
Michael Zito/SportsChrome — Cover
La Salle University — Pages 6, 13
Topps Chewing Gum, Inc. — Page 7 (©1981)
Kobe Japanese Steak House — Page 8
Villanova Sports Information — Page 12
Temple University — Page 15
The following images are from the collection of Team Stewart:
The Upper Deck Company — Pages 28 (© 1994), 40 (© 1996)
Time Inc. — Pages 11 (© 1998), 47 (© 1999)

Printed in the United States of America

Published by
The Millbrook Press, Inc.
2 Old New Milford Road
Brookfield, Connecticut   06804

http://www.millbrookpress.com

Library of Congress Cataloging-in-Publication Data

Stewart, Mark.
    Kobe Bryant: hard to the hoop / by Mark Stewart
    p.   cm.   — (Basketball's new wave)
    Includes index.
    Summary: Discusses the personal life and basketball career of the guard for the Los Angeles Lakers who
became the youngest player in the NBA in 1996.
    ISBN 0-7613-1800-3 (lib. bdg.)   ISBN 0-7613-1380-X (pbk.)
    1. Bryant, Kobe, 1978–   —Juvenile literature. Basketball players—United States—Biography—
Juvenile literature. [1. Bryant, Kobe, 1978–   . 2. Basketball players. 3. Afro-Americans—Biography.]
I. Title. II. Series.
GV884.B794 S74 2000
796.323'092--dc21
[B]   99-046222

pbk: 1 3 5 7 9 10 8 6 4 2
lib: 1 3 5 7 9 10 8 6 4 2

Contents

Chapter	Page
1 Basketball in His Blood	.5
2 La Dolce Vita	.9
3 Home Again	.14
4 Senior Sensation	.19
5 The Kid Can Play	.25
6 Sixth Man	.31
7 Stepping Up	.36
8 Welcome to Reality	.42
Index	.48

Basketball in His Blood

chapter **1**

"Joe could do just about anything with a basketball."
— DEL HARRIS, NBA COACH

On the playgrounds of Philadelphia, the old-timers still talk about "Jellybean," the 6-foot 9-inch (206-cm) sharpshooter with silky smooth moves and outrageous jumping ability. Back in the early 1970s, Joe Bryant was a man ahead of his time, a point guard in a power forward's body. He also was one of the few blacktop stars who were able to ride their basketball talents out of the ghetto and into a better life.

After graduating from John Bartram High School in 1972, Joe accepted a scholarship at nearby La Salle University. There he averaged 10 rebounds and 20 points a game, and most important, met the future Mrs. Bryant. Her name was Pam Cox, and Joe caught her eye at a college doubleheader held at the Palestra in Philadelphia. She was there to watch her brother, John, play for Villanova.

Pam recognized Joe from years before. Their grandparents had lived on the same block, and they would occasionally see each other during family visits. Joe had once bragged to his friends that he would marry Pam one day. She and Joe fell in love and were soon married.

When high-school star Kobe Bryant announced that he planned to go pro in the spring of 1996, he followed in the footsteps of his father, Joe.

Joe Bryant was a big star for La Salle.

Joe decided to take his talents to the NBA after his junior year at La Salle, and he was drafted by the Golden State Warriors in the first round. So began a basketball odyssey for Joe and Pam Bryant that ended up right back in Philadelphia some 16 years later, when the big fellow hung up his sneakers and accepted a job as an assistant coach at La Salle. In between, the Bryants raised three children, lived in three countries, and learned a lot about life, love, and the ups and downs of professional sports.

Their youngest child, Kobe, grew up surrounded by basketball. By the time he was ready to step out of his father's shadow and into the spotlight, he knew more about the game than most players twice his age. He, too, was long and lean, and like Joe he packed a point guard's skills into a forward's body. But unlike his father, whose unusual combination of size and skill made him an NBA misfit, Kobe is considered by many to be basketball's next great player.

Joe's first lesson about the realities of pro basketball came right after the draft, when the Warriors refused his salary demands and sold him to the Philadelphia 76ers. He welcomed this deal, because it meant that he and Pam—and their first child, Sharia—would be among friends and family when he started his career. The 76ers were an improving team with a mix of veterans and young players. The youngest was 18-year-

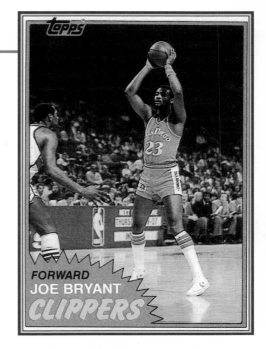

FORWARD
JOE BRYANT
CLIPPERS

old Darryl Dawkins, who was only the second player ever to bypass college and go straight from high school to the pros. Joe played about 15 minutes a game for the 76ers, mostly at forward and center. Coach Gene Shue did not consider using him at guard, but that was all right with Joe. He was just happy to be in the league and cashing a regular paycheck.

Just before Joe's fourth season with Philadelphia, on August 23, 1978, Pam gave birth to Kobe. In 1979, Joe was traded to the San Diego Clippers. San Diego was a great place to raise kids. The weather was great, people were friendly, and Kobe and his sisters, Sharia and Shaya, could play outside all day. Joe was the team's "sixth man," chipping in about 10 points and 5 rebounds a game off the bench. Kobe first got into basketball while his dad played for the Clippers, and by the age of three he began telling anyone who would listen that he would also be a big star in the NBA.

The next stop for the Bryants was Houston, as Joe was dealt to the Rockets right after the 1981–1982 season. The team was horrible, although Joe played well as the Rockets' sixth man. Joe also struck up a friendship with coach Del Harris, whose teaching skills he greatly admired.

Kobe does not remember much about Houston. The family was there for

Did You Know?

Kobe has loved the purple-and-gold Los Angeles uniform longer than he can remember. His parents have pictures of him wearing a toddler's Laker warm-up jacket.

just one year. But it is a good bet that he spent much of his time bouncing a basketball. It was four-year-old Kobe's favorite thing to do. "From day one I was dribbling," he remembers.

One of the players Kobe liked to copy was Earvin "Magic" Johnson, the dynamic young 6-9 point guard. Joe smiled when he saw his son idolizing Magic, but it had to

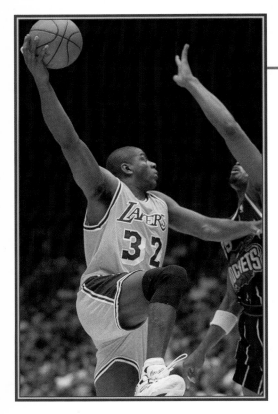

Magic Johnson revolutionized the guard position during the 1980s by proving a big man could play on the perimeter.

hurt a little, too. The NBA had suddenly "discovered" the value of playing a big man at the guard position, thanks to the Lakers' superstar. When Joe had unveiled his end-to-end rushes and no-look passes years earlier in Philadelphia, he was criticized for being undisciplined and playing "street ball." Now everyone wanted a big guard who could make flashy plays. Sadly, it was too late for Joe. He had bulked up in order to play on the front line, and at the age of 30 had lost his blazing speed.

After the 1982–1983 season, the Rockets informed Joe that they would not be renewing his contract for the following year. He picked up the phone and began calling around, but no one in the NBA seemed interested in offering him a job. Joe and Pam had a decision to make. He could begin looking for a coaching job in the United States, or he could follow the path many players had taken and play professionally in Europe. Had Joe been single, he might have stayed in the United States and tried to catch on with an NBA team. But you cannot take chances with three little mouths to feed. So Joe signed with a team in Rieti, Italy. For the next few years, those little mouths would be eating a lot of pasta!

Kobe got his name from a Japanese steakhouse in the Philadelphia suburb of King of Prussia. Joe Bryant liked the sound of the name.

La Dolce Vita

chapter 1

> *"We really began to rely heavily on each other because we were all we had."*
> — KOBE'S SISTER SHARIA

Joe Bryant was a little nervous about playing in Italy. There were the differences in customs, food, and, of course, language. He worried that the schedule might throw him off. Italian teams practice twice a day, but play just once a week. Also, much would be expected of him—and he knew from others who had played in European leagues that the fans could get pretty nasty if you failed to meet their expectations.

Did You Know?

Kobe's parents would not let him watch scary or violent shows on television. *"Growing up it was all BABES IN TOYLAND and WILLIE WONKA AND THE CHOCOLATE FACTORY,"* he says. *"Those are things kids should be exposed to. You don't need to see all this violence."*

In many ways, the Bryant children faced even greater challenges. They were all learning how to read and write, but before they could do that they would have to learn Italian! They decided to do it as a team.

"My two sisters and I got together after school to teach each other the words we had learned," says Kobe. "I was able to speak Italian pretty well within a few months."

While his children were making their way in school, Joe was finally able to display all of his talents. He became one of the big stars of Italian basketball. He would regularly score 30 to 40 points a game, and bring the crowd to its feet with thunderous dunks and impossible behind-the-back passes.

Kobe loved having a famous father. At the same time he began to understand that, when you are a star, your life is not entirely your own. "I'd say back then, 'I don't want to go through that,'" Kobe recalls. But he also remembers how thrilled fans were when they did see Joe. "When you do go out, you've got the opportunity to make people's day, because people want to see you. For whatever reason, they want to see you, they want to meet you. That's a great opportunity for you to put a smile on their faces."

Kobe's weekly routine revolved around his father's basketball schedule. There was a game every Sunday, and occasionally one on a Wednesday or

The Catchings sisters—Tamika (top) and Tauja (bottom)—were childhood friends of Kobe's.

NBA fans have Joe Bryant to thank every time they see Kobe's smiling face on a magazine cover. "My father always played with a great love of the game, and that's one thing he always taught me," says Kobe. "I think that's the best advice anyone's ever given me."

Thursday. On Saturdays, after practice, Joe would lead the family on a hiking or sightseeing adventure. On Mondays—Joe's day off—he would take the family to one of the big cities and meet with the families of other Americans playing in Italy. Shaya and Sharia especially liked the daughters of Harvey Catchings, a former teammate of Joe's on the 76ers. Tauja and Tamika Catchings are now top players in their own right.

During the week, Joe would come home from morning practice and eat lunch. Then he would pick Kobe up from school and take him to afternoon practice. While the team went through its drills, Kobe would shoot by himself in a corner of the gym, trying to copy his dad's moves. During games, Kobe would wander onto the court at halftime and shoot baskets for the fans. "The crowd would be cheering me," he remembers. "I loved it."

Soon Kobe was challenging the players on his father's team. They would usually let him win, but Kobe never knew it. He gained great confidence from those one-on-one "victories," and it made him feel wonderful to do well with his dad shouting encouragement from the sidelines.

Kobe may have been 3,500 miles (5,633 km) from the nearest NBA teams, but he got to see them play whenever he wanted to, thanks to his grandparents. They would videotape the games and send packages to Italy once or twice a week. Every so often,

Kobe's Uncle "Chubby"—former Villanova star John Cox—helped Joe Bryant refine his son's skills during the family's summer visits to Philadelphia.

they would include a highlight video. Kobe's favorite was *NBA Showmen*, which highlighted some of basketball's all-time greats. From these tapes Kobe learned about the sport's history and the evolution of the game. Joe also received tapes from scouting services in the United States. Father and son would watch the tapes together, and Kobe was amazed at how his dad could predict what was going to happen every time down the floor. During these video sessions, Joe taught Kobe to see the whole court, and understand what all 10 players were doing. Soon, Kobe could "read a game" almost as well as his father.

Just how good a basketball player was Kobe? Because so few kids took the game seriously in Europe, he did not have many opportunities to test himself against quality competition. During the summers, however, the Bryants usually flew back to Philadelphia for a month or two, and while there Kobe was able to compete in the city's high-powered Sonny Hill League. He played each summer from the age of 10, and held his own against boys his age and older. Between games, Kobe's father and uncle became his coaches, smoothing out the wrinkles in his game and teaching him a couple of schoolyard tricks. "My dad and Uncle Chubby spent a lot of time with me," he recalls. "They worked on my shooting, rebounding, and defense. In addition, they encouraged me to play hard all the time."

Aside from playing ball and visiting his grandparents, Kobe did not particularly enjoy his summers in Philadelphia. He had little in common with the other kids, and could not join in conversations about American sports, movies, television, or music. "Living in Italy most of the year, I was somewhat cut off," Kobe explains. "Knowing music is a big part of being a teenager and connecting with other kids."

During the 1991–1992 season, Joe decided it was time to retire from basketball and move back to America. Shaya and Sharia were beginning to think about college, and Kobe was ready to begin high school. Kobe said his *arivadercis* (good-byes) and prepared to continue his basketball career in suburban Philadelphia. His friends wished him luck, but warned him not to be disappointed if he found the going difficult. "They told me, 'You're a great player over here, but when you get over to America, it won't be like that.'"

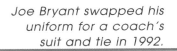
Joe Bryant swapped his uniform for a coach's suit and tie in 1992.

Home Again

chapter }

"As long as I had my basketball there with me, I could escape."
— KOBE BRYANT

Kobe made a smooth transition into American basketball, becoming one of the Sonny Hill League's top players during the summer of 1992. The transition into American life was not as easy. During that first summer, Kobe realized what a sheltered life he had led. Other kids offered him drugs and alcohol, and he witnessed some form of intimidation or violence almost every day. It was scary and confusing. Luckily, Kobe could always say he had a game or a practice and cut out.

"Everywhere I went I went with my sisters. That's the reason our whole family is so tight now."
KOBE BRYANT

Eddie Jones, star of the Temple Owls, befriended Kobe in 1993.

The Bryants moved into a house in the Philadelphia suburb of Ardmore, and Joe took a job as an assistant coach at La Salle. Kobe enrolled at Lower Merion High School and immediately became one of the school's most successful students. He kept a solid B average in the classroom and blew away the competition on the court. In his first two years with the Aces, he consistently scored in the mid-20s and pulled down 10 to 15 rebounds a game. During the summers, he continued to play in the Philadelphia playgrounds. "I knew that playing for Lower Merion I would be facing the best players from the suburban area," Kobe says. "I knew that the Sonny Hill League would give me a chance to face the best players from the city."

Occasionally, Kobe would wander over to the gym at Temple University looking for pickup games. In 1993, he became friendly with Eddie Jones, who starred for the Temple Owls. They played against each other a number of times and became quite friendly. A few years later, they would meet again.

The expert coaching and high-quality competition to which Kobe was exposed as a teenager began paying

Did You Know?

When Kobe made the Lower Merion varsity as a freshman, he selected the jersey number of his idol. "Magic Johnson was my favorite," he says. "I wore Magic's number until my senior year of high school." Kobe switched to number 33 in 1995–1996, when he outgrew the number 32 jersey.

major dividends his junior season at Lower Merion. Kobe was growing 2 to 3 inches (5–8 cm) a year, and no one could be sure how tall he would be once he stopped. But he and Joe decided that no matter how big he got, he definitely would be a guard, so they were always working on the dribbling, passing, and footwork required to play the position. Every time Kobe sprouted an inch or two, he would have to re-learn these skills and adjust to his new body. The talents of high-school stars sometimes fade when they grow quickly, especially when coaches move them to a new position. Lower Merion coach Gregg Downer had no intention of moving Kobe from his spot at shooting guard. And he was thrilled to see him bigger and better after returning each summer from the playgrounds of Philadelphia.

During the 1994–1995 season, Kobe was just fantastic. He averaged 31.1 points, 10.4 rebounds, and 5.2 assists and was named Pennsylvania Player of the Year. Kobe also unveiled his devastating crossover dribble during his junior season. He learned it from God Shammgod, a teammate on his summer AAU squad.

After school let out in the spring of 1995, Kobe began thinking about his future. His grades and test scores were excellent, so he knew he could attend any college in the country on a basketball scholarship. High on his list were Duke, North Carolina, Villanova, and Michigan. The main thing was to keep improving, stay healthy, and remain focused on his goals.

In late June, Kobe began to think very seriously about another option. Kevin Garnett, a 6-11 (211-cm) senior from Chicago's Farragut Academy, was selected in the first round of the NBA draft by the Minnesota Timberwolves, and promptly signed a

deal worth millions of dollars. "He just beat me to the punch," Kobe says of Garnett's move to the NBA. "I'd been thinking about it since the ninth grade."

Garnett was not a good student, and did not see college as an attractive option, so he made himself available to the pros. Still, this intrigued Kobe. "Am I good enough to get drafted?" he wondered. When he first brought up the idea to his parents, they asked him why he would consider skipping college for the NBA. He told them it was

Kevin Garnett was all smiles prior to his first NBA season. Garnett's jump to the pros convinced Kobe to try.

not about money, and obviously he was not frightened by the academic demands of college. Kobe said that he would like to test his skills against the best in the business, and did not know if he would be happy in college knowing he was good enough to be a pro.

That summer, Joe arranged for Kobe to work out with some members of the Philadelphia 76ers. Kobe seemed right at home, and was easily one of the best players on the court. Meanwhile, in his daily one-on-one matches against his dad, Kobe was starting to win regularly.

This time, no one was letting Kobe win. In fact, Joe hated to lose, and he would often resort to terror tactics when the games got close. "He was real physical with me," remembers Kobe. "He'd elbow me in the mouth, rip my lip open. Then my mother would walk out on the court and the elbows would stop."

Joe began to think that Kobe might indeed be ready for the pros. He already had the intelligence and toughness. Who knows? In a year, his son might very well have the skills to jump directly to the NBA.

The Bryant File

KOBE'S FAVORITE...

Movie . . . . *Star Wars*
Hobbies . . . . Swimming, dancing, writing poetry and rap lyrics
Country . . . . Italy; he vacations there each summer.
Food . . . . Pasta and apple pie
Meal . . . . Breakfast; on road trips, he orders breakfast three times a day.
Football Player . . . . . Emmitt Smith
Baseball Player . . . . . . Hank Aaron
Cartoon Character . . . . Road Runner
Actress . . . . Jennifer Love Hewitt
Actor . . . . Jack Nicholson
Singer . . . . Alanis Morissette
Way to Relax . . . . Playing Nintendo on his 85-inch (216-cm) TV. "The characters are like, lifesize. It's weird, man."

Kobe has the same philosophy for success in basketball and in life. "You have to work hard. You have to continue to stay aggressive, regardless of what people say and people do. You have to continue to be yourself."

Senior Sensation

chapter 4

"I have decided to skip college and take my talents to the NBA."

— KOBE BRYANT

Kobe returned to the court as a senior and was unstoppable. He scored at will, made incredible passes, went high above the rim for rebounds, and played superb defense. Kobe's play put Lower Merion on the high-school basketball map. The school's name was in the newspapers constantly, college coaches filled the stands for every game, and Coach Downer received invitations to several prestigious tournaments.

Did You Know?

In high school, Kobe won a slam-dunk contest by jumping over three teammates and jamming the ball in the basket.

*The opportunity to play against all-time greats Magic Johnson (left) and
Michael Jordan (right) was too good for Kobe to pass up.*

As Lower Merion marched toward a 32–3 record and its first state title in 42 years,
Kobe began to lean toward going pro. His two favorite players—Michael Jordan and
Magic Johnson—had both come out of retirement and rejoined the NBA. "I wanted
to get in the league and play against those guys!" smiles Kobe.

Kobe finished his senior year with a scoring average of 30.8 points per game. For
his high-school career, he averaged 29.3 points per game and totaled 2,883 points to
demolish the record set four decades earlier by a Philadelphia schoolboy named Wilt
Chamberlain. Once the season ended, the craziness began, as everyone waited for
Kobe's decision. Would he turn pro, or would he make some college coach the happi-
est man on the planet?

That spring, Kobe called a press conference in the Lower Merion gym. Dozens of
reporters and camera crews jammed into the building, jostling for position as Kobe—
with ultracool shades perched atop his shaved head—loped up to the podium. With
friends from the group Boyz II Men backing him up, he announced that he had decided
to take his talents to the NBA.

*Lower Merion coach Gregg Downer watches as Kobe signs
autographs following his April 29 press conference in the school's gym.*

*Kobe shared the spotlight at his senior prom with his date,
TV and singing star Brandy Norwood.*

Over the next few weeks, the newspapers and airwaves were filled with conjecture
and opinions. Some said Kobe was crazy. Others said he had made a brilliant decision.
A lot of people who did not know Joe and Pam Bryant attacked Kobe's parents for letting their son pass up an education. At every opportunity, Kobe defended his mom and
dad, and patiently explained his decision.

"I look at basketball from the same perspective as a kid who wants to major in biolo-
gy," he says. "He would go to college to learn from the best biologists out there. It's the
same with me and basketball. Who better to learn from than the best players in the world?"

Ready for the
Big Time

"He may be the most skilled guard to come out of Philadelphia, and probably the whole East Coast, in many years.
BOB GIBBONS, RECRUITING EXPERT

"This is a uniquely nice kid, but also a uniquely talented kid."
JERRY WEST, NBA HALL OF FAMER

"Kobe's a well-balanced young man. He's always stayed focused on what is important. I don't worry with Kobe or any of my children, because we have a good family foundation."
PAM BRYANT, KOBE'S MOTHER

"I'm still young, still only 17, but I'm a man on the court. I feel I have the maturity of someone who's 21 or 22."
KOBE BRYANT

The Kid Can Play

"The whole season was just an ongoing learning process."
— KOBE BRYANT

As the 1996 NBA draft neared, a lot of teams had to make a decision on Kobe. The top four picks in the draft would likely be Marcus Camby, Allen Iverson, Stephon Marbury, and Ray Allen. But from there, the college talent thinned quickly. Was Kobe worth a "lottery" pick? Did he deserve to be in the first 10? It was impossible to say. No one with his combination of size, skill, and age had ever been available before.

The Los Angeles Lakers liked Kobe a lot. In this young man they saw someone who understood what the life of a pro basketball player was all about. They saw someone who appreciated the game, and had studied its roots and its history. The fact that Kobe did not come from a poor family—and was a smart kid—made team owner Jerry Buss and president Jerry West believe that he would have the patience to improve gradually, where

A month before the 1996 NBA draft, Kobe already had a sneaker deal with adidas.

The tension mounted as Kobe wondered which club would select him in the draft. NBA Commissioner David Stern congratulates 10th pick Erick Dampier. Kobe was taken with the 13th pick.

a more desperate and less intelligent high-schooler might not. They also liked Kobe's maturity and his grasp of basketball's fundamentals, which most young players do not possess.

There was, of course, never any question about Kobe's ability. In a workout for the Lakers, West asked Kobe to jump and touch as high as he could on the backboard. The entire Los Angeles front office watched open-mouthed as Kobe sprang into the air and slapped the *top* of the board with his fingers.

The Lakers were sold on Kobe. The only problem was that L.A. owned the 24th pick in the draft, and West knew Kobe would not last that long. When the Charlotte Hornets grabbed him with the 13th pick, West hatched a plan. First, he used the team's first-round pick on Derek Fisher, a defensive-minded point guard out of Arkansas–Little Rock. Next, he traded the Hornets a proven center, Vlade Divac, for Kobe. Finally, with the extra salary space created by Divac's departure, West was then able to sign Shaquille O'Neal. Shaq had become a superstar for the Orlando Magic and had taken

Did You Know?

After watching 18-year-old Kobe perform a miraculous move during practice, teammate Elden Campbell told him, "You should have come out after 11th grade!"

them to the NBA finals, but he yearned for the bright lights of Los Angeles.

Kobe could not have been more pleased. He was starting his pro career with his favorite team, and the Lakers already had exceptional talent, which meant he could learn and improve at his own pace. Besides Shaq, there was point guard Nick Van

Kobe erased any doubt that he could hold his own with the pros during the summer of 1996.

Exel, power forward Elden Campbell, and his old pal, shooting guard Eddie Jones. As an added bonus, Del Harris was the team's coach—talk about a small world!

Kobe joined the Lakers' summer-league team and competed against pros from the Suns, Grizzlies, Warriors, and Clippers. Any doubts that he could compete on this level were erased by the end of August, when he finished with an average of 25 points per game. "The fact I played well didn't convince me I was ready to play in the NBA," says Kobe. "I was convinced before that. I felt I could have played a lot better. And if I hadn't played well in the summer, it still would have been a positive. It would have simply been a way of telling me what I had to work on. I would have just gone back to the gym and worked on my weaknesses."

It turned out that Kobe's main weakness was his judgment. When you play basketball for a living, you have certain responsibilities, and one of them is staying healthy. Despite signing a three-year, $3.5 million contract and a lucrative endorsement deal

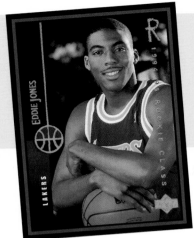

Two years before Kobe's arrival in Los Angeles, the city's hottest rookie card belonged to his pal Eddie Jones. Jones advised him to stop playing street ball after he signed with the Lakers, but he did not listen. "When you get to L.A.," he told Kobe, "stay away from these playgrounds."

with adidas, Kobe was still playing ball in the playgrounds. A game was a game, as far as he was concerned. As far as his playground opponents were concerned, here was a chance to prove yourself against basketball's most famous teenager. Kobe was hacked, tripped, shoved, and elbowed every time he stepped on the court. Yet it never occurred to him that he might be jeopardizing his career. During a Labor Day pickup game at Venice Beach, Kobe fractured his left wrist. Luckily, it was not a serious injury. But it meant he would have to sit out five weeks, and miss much of his first training camp with the Lakers. He would not make this mistake again.

Kobe made his official NBA debut in the first quarter of the season opener against the Minnesota Timberwolves. He missed his only shot and committed a turnover, but also hauled down a rebound and blocked a shot.

Coach Harris used Kobe carefully during the first part of the 1996–1997 season. He put him into situations where he thought he could succeed, and kept him out of games when Kobe's inexperience or exuberance might lead to a mistake. Because the Lakers were winning most of their ball games, there was no need to rush Kobe into the starting lineup.

In February of his rookie year, Kobe was selected to compete in the Slam Dunk Contest at the NBA All-Star Game. Normally, a guy averaging under 10 points and 2 rebounds never gets anywhere near this event. But the league saw how enthusiastically young fans responded to Kobe, and wanted to give him as much exposure as he could handle. Kobe loved being a part of All-Star Weekend. Some of the game's all-time greats were there, and he got a chance to meet many of the players whom he had watched on his highlight videos as a kid. Kobe also played in the Rookie All-Star Game and set a record with 31 points.

When the Slam Dunk Contest finally started, Kobe was pumped up. He flew through the air and hammered the ball in from all different angles, making up dunks as he went. His big finale was a mind-bending, between-the-legs windmill jam that won the contest. "You have to have a lot of things in your bag you can pull out," he says of his repertoire. "You might practice certain things, but all the really good moves are spontaneous. I tried to be as competitive as possible and use my instincts on the way up to the rim. It felt great to win. Winning the dunk contest is something I dreamed about since I was a little kid."

The rest of the season was not as much fun. Injuries to O'Neal and other key players killed the Lakers, and they limped through just one round of the playoffs before being eliminated. Kobe finished the year averaging slightly more than 15 minutes and 7 points a game. "You get a little upset when you don't get the big minutes," he says, looking back. "But you've got to learn to wait your turn."

Shaquille O'Neal (left) took Kobe under his wing when he joined the team. When Shaq came out of games to rest, he tried to explain the finer points of the NBA game to Kobe.

Sixth Man

"I'll do whatever it takes to win games, whether it's sitting on a bench waving a towel, handing a cup of water to a teammate, or hitting the game-winning shot."

— KOBE BRYANT

Prior to the 1997–1998 season, Jerry West and Del Harris decided they wanted Kobe to be the team's new "sixth man." This is an important role in the NBA. As the first player off the bench, the sixth man must watch the game carefully, get a feel for its flow and tempo, and then determine how he can have the greatest possible impact once he enters. These were all the things Kobe's father had taught him!

Kobe played his role perfectly. He was dynamite off the bench, averaging nearly 18 points per game and playing between 20 and 30 minutes a night. He was just the spark the Lakers needed, and they reeled off 11 straight victories to start the year.

The better Kobe did, the more attention the league focused on him. He was a bright story in an otherwise difficult season. Attendance was dropping at NBA games,

Del Harris—Joe Bryant's last NBA coach—was Kobe's first. He says he saw a lot of Joe in his young star.

Michael Jordan was playing his final season, Lattrell Sprewell of the Warriors made headlines when he choked his coach, and the possibility of a labor dispute loomed in the distance. When fans voted Kobe into the starting lineup at the 1998 All-Star Game, the NBA seized on this opportunity and began advertising the contest as a battle between the NBA's past (Jordan) and its future (Kobe).

Did You Know?

At 19, Kobe was the youngest All-Star in league history. During All-Star Weekend, he was besieged by interview requests and honored as many as he could, from **MTV** to **MEET THE PRESS**.

Unfortunately, all the hype and publicity got to Kobe. Worse, he chose the All-Star Game to challenge Jordan one-on-one! Kobe made the highlight shows with a team-high 18 points—including a spectacular 360° tomahawk dunk—but in the end, Jordan destroyed Kobe at both ends of the floor. By the third quarter, Kobe's Western Conference teammates were getting angry, feeling he was hogging the ball. On one play, veteran Karl Malone tried to set a pick for Kobe. Kobe motioned for him to get out of the way. It was the height of self-

ishness and disrespect. Eventually, coach George Karl took the teenager out and sat him on the bench for the final quarter.

Kobe did not understand what he had done wrong. He thought the idea of the All-Star Game was to have fun and entertain the fans. The NBA had been running newspaper ads for the event with a full-page picture of Kobe next to a full-page picture of Jordan. He figured the league expected him to deliver on its promise to the fans. "It was like they were making it out to be some big one-on-

Michael Jordan showed Kobe he had a lot to learn on his way to earning MVP honors at the 1998 NBA All-Star Game.

Karl Malone led the Jazz past the Lakers in the 1998 playoffs. Kobe describes the experience as "humbling."

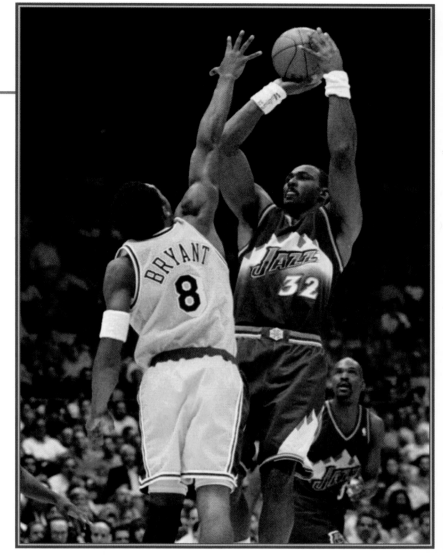

one showdown," Kobe remembers. "I'd do it all over again. I had a blast in that game. I'm sorry if some guys didn't like it, but this is who I am. I was just being aggressive."

The most important lesson Kobe learned from his All-Star experience was actually from Jordan, who took him aside and gave him some advice. "It's important to stay aggressive," the superstar told Kobe. "You have to continue to be aggressive."

Kobe faced his first major adjustment as a pro during the latter half of his second season. Opponents had analyzed his game and devised special defensive maneuvers to stop him. When he shook his man and veered toward the basket, there was no longer an open lane—in fact, an even bigger player was usually waiting for him. Kobe did not pass off quickly enough in these situations, and sometimes did not pass at all. He forced shots he could not make, and he began to hurt the team. Coach Harris punished Kobe for his poor play, reducing his time on the court. He told Kobe that it was fine to want to be like Michael Jordan, but pointed out that Jordan no longer looked to make spectacular plays. He looked to make *winning* plays. "His highlight films are of him kissing a trophy," Harris liked to remind Kobe.

Though frustrated, Kobe knew that this was part of the growing-up process—a process that continues to this day. "I *want* to go through periods when I'm struggling," he says, "because that's when you learn. And the more you learn the better you get."

Kobe got the message and cleaned up his act. By season's end he was getting quality minutes again, and the Lakers were going to him in key situations.

The Lakers went into the 1998 postseason with a lot of talent, but without much experience. In the season's final weeks, they had lost a lot of close games—games you need to win in order to build confidence. It was the mark of a young team. "I think we all needed to show more poise," recalls Kobe, who is quick to identify himself as one of the chief culprits. "Sometimes I would go on pure instinct instead of thinking about the play unfolding."

The Lakers pulled together and made it all the way to the Western Conference finals. But that was where their season ended. The Utah Jazz, one of the league's most poised and experienced clubs, demolished Los Angeles. In the final game, the Lakers

had a chance to win, and Kobe had the ball in his hands with time running out. Instead of working it into Shaq, Kobe fired a long jumper that missed everything. In the ensuing overtime period, he shot three more air balls in critical situations. As the team left the court in defeat, it dawned on Kobe that he was a lot farther away from playing championship basketball than he had thought. "It was humbling," he remembers.

"When younger guys tell me to get out of the way, that's a game I don't need to be in."
KARL MALONE

Mr. Moves

When it comes to expanding his repertoire of offensive moves, Kobe says he is like a computer that stores and retrieves information. His teammates agree.

"I've never seen anybody who can see a move that another guy does and pick it up as quickly as he can," says Robert Horry. "He'll work on it and two days later you'll see it in his game."

Kobe makes sure to copy from the all-time greats. He says he got his spin from Earl Monroe, his one-on-one moves from Pete Maravich, his fall-away jumper from Hakeem Olajuwon, and his baseline jumper from Oscar Robertson. "I really try to borrow things from every player," Kobe explains. "Magic Johnson, how he dishes the ball, Michael Jordan's post-up or whatever it might be, Reggie Miller's step-back. Little pieces and bits from every player, I'll take it and add it to my game."

Stepping Up

chapter 7

> *"I hope everyone realizes that once we let Kobe into the starting lineup, we'll never get him out."*
> — JERRY WEST

During the summer of 1998, the players and owners began negotiating a new working agreement. The players were happy to keep things the way they were. The owners were not. The dispute dragged on for months, with neither side willing to back down. NBA commissioner David Stern came very close to canceling the season. Finally, the owners gave in a little and the players gave in a lot, and the season was saved. The lockout ended in time for the NBA to schedule an abbreviated 50-game season.

> *"He has the ability to read, visualize, and anticipate."*
> KURT RAMBIS

Kobe was not afraid to speak out against the deal the players accepted to save the 1999 NBA season. He thought they had given in. Many believe Kobe will assume a major role in the players' union when he gets older.

The 1999 season held great promise for the Lakers. The Chicago Bulls, winners of three straight NBA titles, were no longer the league's dominant team. Michael Jordan had retired, Scottie Pippen was playing for the Rockets, and Dennis Rodman had declared himself a free agent. For the Lakers to take the next step forward and challenge for the championship, Kobe eventually would have to move into a starting role and become a team leader.

His chance to step up came much sooner than anyone thought. On opening night, forward Rick Fox was removed from the lineup because of a problem with the special inserts he wears in his shoes. Kobe took his place against the Houston Rockets and lit

Kobe served notice that he was ready to start when he overwhelmed Scottie Pippen early in 1999.

them up for 25 points and 10 rebounds. He also bottled up Pippen, limiting him to just 10 points. "It was a big game for me personally," remembers Kobe, who says that his performance against Pippen all but gave him the starting job. "I think, looking back on my career, when it's all said and done, I'll say it sped up the process. It was a fun night."

Kobe needed to make some mental adjustments in order to remain an effective starter. As a sixth man, his job had been to ignite the team by coming off the bench, create matchup problems for opponents, and score quick points. As a starter, he no longer had to change the tempo of a game, he had to help *establish* it. This meant creating more opportunities for teammates, and being more patient when he had the ball in his hands.

Kobe progressed quickly during the first half of the season, and worked well with point guards Derek Fisher and Derek Harper. Kobe averaged just under 20 points a game, and was among the team leaders in points,

Did You Know?

Kobe works especially well with point guard Derek Fisher. As the team's backup guards, they had played together constantly in games and practices for two years.

rebounds, assists, and steals. He did this under trying circumstances, as the Lakers went through several major upheavals. Wild and crazy Dennis Rodman joined the team early in the year, and Del Harris was dismissed after just 12 games. His replacement, Kurt Rambis, was a big supporter of Kobe's, but it was not easy to get used to a new coach. Then Los Angeles made a mega-deal with the Hornets, sending longtime Lakers Elden Campbell and Eddie Jones to Charlotte for Glen Rice. The pickup of Rice created more room for Kobe to maneuver. Rice, a great long-distance shooter, could draw enemy defenders out to the perimeter, making it harder to double-team Kobe when he slashed to the basket.

Every so often, the Lakers would get a glimpse of the player Kobe will someday be. In a March game against the Orlando Magic, he spent the first half moving the ball around and playing smothering defense. In the second half, when the team needed an offensive boost, he simply took over, making 13 of 16 shots and scoring 33 points. His game total of 38 was his best as a pro. In a late-season game against the Warriors, Kobe played the role of "comeback kid." The Lakers were down by 28 points, and Shaq had been ejected. Instead of trying to get all those points back at once, Kobe calmly stepped up his game and patiently brought the Lakers back within striking distance. In the final quarter, he turned on the afterburners and scored 16 points to send the game

Kobe gets a step on Matt Harpring in a 1999 game against the Orlando Magic. Kobe scored a career-high 38 points in a 115–104 win.

into overtime. After the contest, which Los Angeles won, Kobe realized he had taken a big step in his career. "My father told me I had to learn how to take over a game 'quietly,'" Kobe says. "I didn't know what he meant until after that game."

The Lakers dueled right down to the wire with the Portland Trail Blazers for supremacy in the NBA's Pacific Division. Basketball fans found this race very interesting, for it pitted two completely different teams against each other. The Trail Blazers were a club of highly talented role players, with a coach (Mike Dunleavy) who moved them around like chess pieces. There was no one star on the team, no "go-to guy." The Lakers, on the other hand, were a team with three "go-to guys"—Shaq, Kobe, and Rice.

Kobe found himself in a complicated situation. As his game improved, Coach Rambis expected him to do more each night. But this caused jealousy on the part of some teammates, especially when Kobe tried to do *too* much and made mistakes. Shaquille O'Neal, a good friend during Kobe's rookie year, actually became a rival as the spotlight began to shift to Kobe. Shaq was hurt when he realized he was no longer the favorite player of Los Angeles fans. For much of the year, he and Kobe only spoke when necessary.

As the season drew to a close and the Lakers prepared for the playoffs, the tension was so thick in the locker room that you could have cut it with a knife. The players called a meeting to solve their differences and bring some harmony to the club in time for the postseason. A major topic was the team's treatment of Kobe. Everyone agreed that they would try to remember how young he was, and they would encourage him as much as possible.

Kobe finished the season among the NBA's Top 20 in scoring and minutes played. He averaged 19.9 points, 5.3 rebounds, 3.8 assists, 1.4 steals, and 1.0 blocks per game. The Lakers ended up 31–19, four games behind Portland.

The first round of the playoffs found the Lakers taking on the Houston Rockets. The series was billed as a "passing of the torch," as Shaq did battle against

The moment Kobe became a starter, collectors began stockpiling his rookie cards, which tripled in value almost overnight.

> *"This kid has tremendous athletic ability, he has a lot of poise, and he's grown tremendously."*
> UTAH JAZZ PRESIDENT FRANK LAYDEN

veteran Hakeem Olajuwon, and Kobe was matched up with six-time world champion Scottie Pippen. Shaq overpowered Olajuwon, and Kobe played smothering defense on Pippen in three of the four games, as the Lakers advanced with a 3–1 series victory.

In round two, the Lakers ran into the red-hot San Antonio Spurs. After dropping the first game, the Lakers battled back and seemed in control of Game Two. With 19 seconds left, Kobe stood at the foul line with a chance to put his team up by three points. Incredibly, he missed both shots, which allowed the Spurs to come back and score the winning basket. The Lakers let the next game slip away in the fourth quarter, too. And in Game Four, the Spurs—led by Tim Duncan and David Robinson—put Los Angeles away for an embarrassing four-game sweep. San Antonio went on to win the NBA title, but that did not make the Lakers feel any better. Had they limited their mistakes and made a few clutch baskets, they might have been the team to go all the way.

pro *stats*

Season	Team	G	FG%	Reb	Assists	Points
1996–1997	Lakers	71	41.7	1.9	1.3	7.6
1997–1998	Lakers	79	42.8	3.1	2.5	15.4
1998–1999	Lakers	50	46.5	5.3	3.8	19.9
Totals/Averages		**200**	**43.9**	**3.2**	**2.4**	**13.8**

career *highlights*

High School Player of the Year	1996
Youngest Player to Start NBA Game	1996
NBA Slam Dunk Champion	1997
NBA All-Star	1998
Third Team All-NBA	1999

Welcome to Reality

chapter 8

"There hasn't been one minute I've been sorry I did this."
— KOBE BRYANT

ou might think that being the hottest young player in the NBA is nothing but fun. But, as Kobe has begun to realize, it can be frustrating and lonely. As well as his parents prepared him for this life, there were some hard realities that he had to discover for himself. For instance, Kobe was shocked by the problems that developed with Shaquille O'Neal. He thought they would become closer as Kobe got better, but that was not the case. Part of the problem was jealousy on Shaq's part, but much of the blame lay with Kobe.

Kobe's one-on-one moves often leave opponents tripping over their own feet. To reach the next level, he must now work on his passing and defense.

The Lakers' offense must run through its center to be most effective, and it is hard for Kobe to pass up good scoring opportunities in order to work the ball into the post. When your two stars do not see eye-to-eye, it is hard to win consistently.

Is it too late to make up with Shaq? Not at all. If they can get together on the court, they will come together off it. Kobe thinks that, when they perfect the pick-and-roll play, it will be the most lethal weapon in the NBA. "We're going to do it," he predicts. "We do it right and there's nothing anybody could do. Have Shaq sharpen the ax and then let me swing it."

Magic Johnson, who spoke with Shaq and Kobe several times during the 1999 season, believes that the Lakers will not bond as a team until Kobe starts hanging out with his teammates off the court. During his first three NBA seasons, Kobe was under age, and thus was not invited to join their off-court activities. The Lakers like to take advantage of all that Los Angeles has to offer. Players often go from restaurants to private parties to nightclubs togeth-

Working the ball inside to teammates for easy baskets is one of the biggest challenges a big guard like Kobe faces.

er, and over the course of a season they can become very close. Kobe was under 21 his first three years in the NBA, and therefore could not tag along on these adventures. After each game, Kobe would return to the home he shares with his parents and disappear into his room until the next morning. "I go home with my mother, my father, or

Richard Hamilton led UConn to a national title before turning pro with the Washington Wizards in 1999. He and Kobe are good friends.

my sisters," Kobe says of his post-game routine. "We have a nice little dinner together. Then I go to sleep."

Another thing that gets Kobe down is that he was unable to make any close friends in Los Angeles during his first three seasons. The only person his age he talked to was Richard Hamilton, who entered the University of Connecticut the same year Kobe went pro. Hamilton led the Huskies to the NCAA title in 1999, and their phone conversations during the team's amazing run made Kobe wonder what it might have been like to play in college. "Sometimes I do wonder what college would have been like," he admits. "But I made my decision."

Privacy has been another issue that took Kobe by surprise. If he sees a kid wearing a pair of his adidas KB8 sneakers, he will stop his car, get out, and ask how his game is. But when fans run to *him*, he feels awkward and uncomfortable. In the Lakers dressing room, the crush of reporters drives him crazy. He often dresses by himself in a back room. Kobe believes that he will get used to life in the NBA, and asks that his fans and teammates give him time. He may already have a grown-up game, but he still has some growing up to do.

What lies ahead for Kobe *on* the court? That is a subject of much debate. The Lakers have asked him to adjust to the needs of the team. But as many have pointed out, if Kobe continues to improve this rapidly, the day may soon come when it will make more sense for the Lakers to adjust the team to *him*. Those who compare Kobe to a young Michael Jordan would do well to remember that, during Jordan's early years, he too was criticized for not involving his teammates more. When the Chicago

One of the many challenges Phil Jackson will face as the Lakers' coach will be to help Kobe achieve true superstar status.

Bulls finally stopped standing around watching him—and started feeding off his excellence—they became the most dominant team in all of sports.

Much of the credit for Chicago's turnaround went to Coach Phil Jackson, who made the team's other stars feel that they were more than "support players." Part strategist and part psychologist, Jackson created a confident, tight-knit club and also pushed Jordan higher than even he believed he could go. No one was more delighted than Kobe when the Lakers announced that they had hired Jackson for the 1999–2000 season. If he does with Shaq and Kobe what he did with Michael and Scottie, watch out!

So what is it like to be part of the NBA's next generation of stars? Kobe feels that their successes are hyped way too much, and that too much is made of their failures. "Because of the NBA and how everybody's marketed," he says, "sometimes, some of the little things get blown out of proportion. There are some negative things that we do,

> "A lot of these guys are not worthy and not deserving....They want the money but they don't want the responsibility that comes with the money. Kobe is different. He wants all of it."
>
> MAGIC JOHNSON

and I'm not excusing that or trying to hide it in any kind of way, but I think it's important to understand that people are going to make mistakes. Because we are young, we haven't experienced life's lessons yet. It's not like we're perfect."

Kobe also feels that NBA fans are a little alarmed by the hip-hop, in-your-face attitude of today's young stars. He has to smile at that. "This generation is bringing a different type of flow to the NBA," explains Kobe. "A lot of people around the league are not used to it, particularly off the court. The style of dress is different. The way we relate to each other is different...you just need to understand that these are a bunch of young guys who love to have fun!"

Kobe cannot think of anything more fun than winning a few NBA championships. Also, he is perfectly willing to let Shaq or Coach Jackson grab the spotlight and lead the Lakers to the title. He knows he can become a leader in other ways, like putting his head down and playing hard. "I never really want to be a vocal leader," Kobe claims. "The way I look at it, you can push a guy for five or ten minutes, but by leading by example it gives the guy no choice but to follow you. He has no choice."

Did You Know?

Kobe breaks in a new pair of adidas basketball shoes every three or four games.

Whatever the future holds for Kobe, he remains focused on one thing: becoming the most complete player possible. "I'm just going to continue to set the high standards I've set for myself since my first year, and continue to grow and mature," he says. "What I'm doing right now, I'm chasing perfection... and if I don't get it, I'm going to get *this* close."

By the age of 21, Kobe had been on the cover of every major sports magazine. This is one of his favorites.

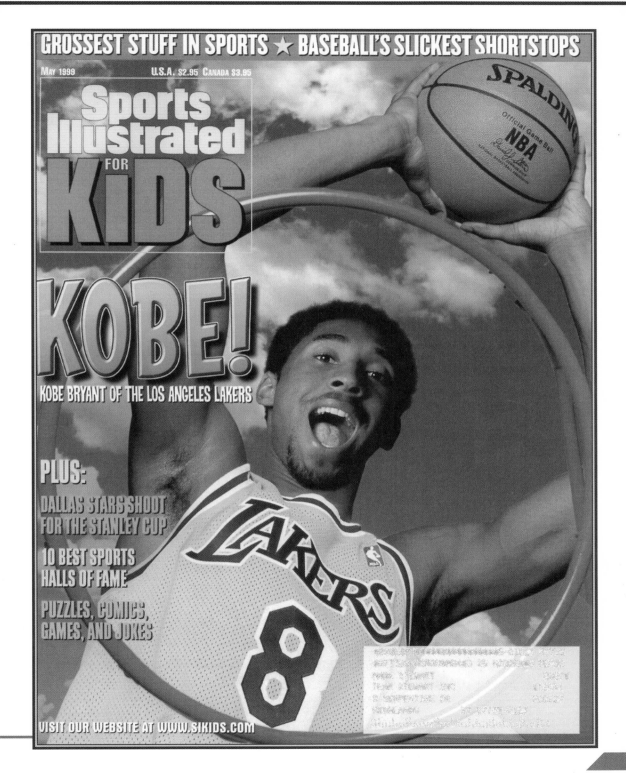

Index

PAGE NUMBERS IN ITALICS REFER TO ILLUSTRATIONS.

Adidas *24*, 27–28
Allen, Ray 25
All-Star Game (1998) 32–33
Bryant, Joe 5–13, *6*, *7*, *13*, 15–18,
   20, 22, 31, 43
Bryant, Kobe *4*, *21*, *35*, *37*
   All-Star Game (1998) 32–33
   baseball cards *40*
   childhood of 6–11
   early basketball 11–13
   endorsements *24*, 27–28
   high school basketball 15–17, 19–20
   with Los Angeles Lakers 26–29, 31–46
   magazine covers *11*, *47*
   NBA draft 25–26
   O'Neal and *29*, 40, 42–43, 45
   professional statistics and
     career highlights 41
   salary 27
Bryant, Pam Cox 5–8, 18, 22, 23, 43
Bryant, Sharia 7, 9–11, 13
Bryant, Shaya 7, 10, 11, 13
Buss, Jerry 25
Camby, Marcus 25
Campbell, Elden 26, 27, 39
Catchings, Harvey 11
Catchings, Tamika *10*, 11
Catchings, Tauja *10*, 11
Chamberlain, Wilt 20
Charlotte Hornets 26, 39
Chicago Bulls 37, 44–45
Cox, Chubby *12*, 12–13
Cox, John 5
Dawkins, Darryl 7
Divac, Vlade 26
Downer, Gregg 16, 19, *21*
Duncan, Tim 41
Dunleavy, Mike 40
Fisher, Derek 26, 38
Fox, Rick 37
Garnett, Kevin 17, *17*
Gibbons, Bob 23
Golden State Warriors 6, 7, 39
Hamilton, Richard 44

Harper, Derek 38
Harpring, Matt 39
Harris, Del 7, 27, 28, *30*, 33–34, 39
Horry, Robert 35
Houston Rockets 7, 8, 37–38, 40–41
Iverson, Allen 25
Jackson, Phil *45*, 45, 46
Johnson, Earvin "Magic" 8, 8, 13, 15,
   20, *20*, 35, 43, 46, *46*
Jones, Eddie *15*, 27, *28*, 28, 39
Jordan, Michael *20*, 20, *32*, 32–35, 37, 44–45
Karl, George 32
La Salle University 5, 6
Layden, Frank 41, *41*
Los Angeles Lakers 23, 26–29, 31–46
Malone, Karl 32, *33*, *34*, 34
Maravich, Pete 35
Marbury, Stephon 25
Miller, Reggie 35
Minnesota Timberwolves 17, 28
Monroe, Earl 35
Norwood, Brandy *22*
Olajuwon, Hakeem 35, 41
O'Neal, Shaquille 26, *29*, 29, 34,
   39–43, 45, 46
Orlando Magic 26, 39–40
Philadelphia 76ers 6–7, 18
Pippen, Scottie 37, *38*, 38, 41, 45
Portland Trailblazers 40
Rambis, Kurt *36*, 36, 39, 40
Rice, Glen 39, 40
Robertson, Oscar 35
Robinson, David 41
Rodman, Dennis 37, 38
San Antonio Spurs 41
San Diego Clippers 7
Shammgod, God *16*, 17
Shue, Gene 7
Sonny Hill League, Philadelphia 12, 14, 15
Sprewell, Lattrell 32
Stern, David 36
Utah Jazz 34
Van Exel, Nick 26–27
West, Jerry 23, 25, 26, 31, 36